Stoney Creek Ontario in Photos, Saving Our History One Photo at a Time

Photography
by Barbara Raué
2012

Series Name:
Cruising Ontario

Book 6: Stoney Creek

Cover photo: Battlefield House taken from Stoney Creek Battlefield Monument

Series Name: Cruising Ontario

Book 1: London
Book 2: Dundas
Book 3: Hamilton
Book 4: Oakville
Book 5: Chesley
Book 6: Stoney Creek
Book 7: Waterdown
Book 8: Owen Sound
Book 9: Mount Forest
Book 10: Dundalk

Other Books by Barbara Raue

Coins and Gems

Arrows, Indians and Love

The Life and Times of Barbara
Volume 1: Inventions That Have Enhanced My Life
Volume 2: Entertainment That I Have Enjoyed
Volume 3: East Coast Trip 2009

Stoney Creek

Stoney Creek is located on the south-western shore of Lake Ontario. It was settled by Loyalists after the American Revolution. The Battle of Stoney Creek during the War of 1812 occurred near Centennial Parkway and King Street. In a surprise night-time attack, the outnumbered British overwhelmed the Americans and forced their retreat to Forty Mile Creek (the present location of Grimsby). In this forty minute battle, hundreds were killed and the two American Generals were captured. Battlefield Park has a monument and museum to preserve the history of this area.

The Nash-Jackson House was originally located at the northeast corner of King Street East and Nash Road in Hamilton. The house was built in 1818 in the Georgian style. The house was moved to Stoney Creek Battlefield Park in 1999.

Battlefield House, 77 King Street West, circa 1796, Georgian style

Battlefield Monument stands 100 feet tall and commemorates a century of peace between the British and the Americans.

The Stoney Creek Dairy Bar, 135 King Street East, opened in 1941 to serve frozen treats. It closed in 2012.

The Powerhouse is a historical landmark at the centre of Stoney Creek, 21 Jones Street. It provided power for electric rail lines in the 1890s. Now it is a restaurant.

15 Jones Street

16 Jones Street

26 King Street

Century Square - 1901

Downtown Stoney Creek

Stoney Creek United Church, 1 King Street, corner of Lake Avenue, founded in 1792

King Street

King Street

10 Lake Avenue

12 Lake Avenue – circa 1890
Former Methodist Parsonage

9 Lake Avenue

14 Lake Avenue

16 Lake Avenue

13 Lake Avenue

18 Lake Avenue

15 Lake Avenue

26 Lake Avenue

28 Lake Avenue

19 Lake Avenue

25 Lake Avenue

27 Lake Avenue

33 Lake Avenue

40 Lake Avenue

42 Lake Avenue – Roubos Greenhouses (garden plants)

39 Lake Avenue

44 Lake Avenue

43 Lake Avenue

46 Lake Avenue

48 Lake Avenue

52 Lake Avenue

53 Lake Avenue

54 Lake Avenue

55 Lake Avenue

57 Lake Avenue

62 Lake Avenue

63 Lake Avenue

89 Lake Avenue – flowering cherry tree to left

72 Lake Avenue – gingerbread trim

91 Lake Avenue

86 Lake Avenue

Stoney Creek Baptist Church – 79 Collegiate Avenue at the corner of Gray Road – built in 1958

91 Donn Avenue – home of Harris and Denise Raue

www.ingramcontent.com/pod-product-compliance
Lightning Source LLC
Chambersburg PA
CBHW061522180526
45171CB00001B/300